I Am
Cooperative

by Sarah L. Schuette

Consulting Editor: Gail Saunders-Smith, Ph.D.

Consultant: Madonna Murphy, Ph.D.
Professor of Education,
University of St. Francis, Joliet, Illinois
Author, *Character Education in America's
Blue Ribbon Schools*

Pebble Books

an imprint of Capstone Press
Mankato, Minnesota

Pebble Books are published by Capstone Press
151 Good Counsel Drive, P.O. Box 669, Mankato, Minnesota 56002
http://www.capstone-press.com

1 2 3 4 5 6 07 06 05 04 03 02

Library of Congress Cataloging-in-Publication Data
Schuette, Sarah L., 1976–
    I am cooperative / by Sarah L. Schuette.
    p. cm.—(Character values)
    Summary: Simple text and photographs show various ways children can
be cooperative.
    ISBN 0-7368-1439-6
    1. Cooperativeness—Juvenile literature. [1. Cooperativeness.] I. Title.
II. Series.
BJ1533.C74 .S34 2003
179'.9—dc21   2001007797

Note to Parents and Teachers

The Character Values series supports national social studies standards for units on individual development and identity. This book describes cooperation and illustrates ways students can be cooperative. The images support early readers in understanding the text. The repetition of words and phrases helps early readers learn new words. This book also introduces early readers to subject-specific vocabulary words, which are defined in the Words to Know section. Early readers may need assistance to read some words and to use the Table of Contents, Words to Know, Read More, Internet Sites, and Index/Word List sections of the book.

Table of Contents

4

I am cooperative. I work with other people.

I cooperate with
my family. I help
my grandparents
with their puzzle.

8

I help my sister clean.

I help set the table
before meals.

I cooperate at school.
I push in my chair.

I help my teacher
hand out paper
when she asks.

16

I work with my friend
on our art project.

18

I work with others
on a team.

I am cooperative.
I do my part.

Words to Know

cooperate—to work with others and to follow rules

follow—to obey; cooperative people follow the rules at home, at school, and in their community without complaining.

help—to assist others; helpful people are cooperative when they volunteer to help someone else.

part—a share of the responsibility for something; doing your part means doing your job.

project—a school assignment that students work on over a period of time

team—a group of people who work together on a project or play a sport together

Read More

Davis, Jennie. *The Child's World of Helping.* Plymouth, Minn.: Child's World, 1998.

Lewis, Barbara A. *Being Your Best: Character Building for Kids 7–10.* Minneapolis: Free Spirit, 2000.

Raatma, Lucia. *Cooperation.* Character Education. Mankato, Minn.: Bridgestone Books, 2000.

Internet Sites

Cooperation
http://library.thinkquest.org/J001709/thinkquest_values/8cooperation/cooperation_frameset.html

Kids Next Door
http://www.hud.gov/kids

Out on a Limb—A Guide to Getting Along
http://www.urbanext.uiuc.edu/conflict

Index/Word List

art, 17
chair, 13
clean, 9
cooperate,
   7, 13
cooperative,
   5, 21
family, 7
friend, 17
grandparents,
   7

hand, 15
help, 7, 9,
   11, 15
meals, 11
others, 19
paper, 15
part, 21
people, 5
project, 17
push, 13
puzzle, 7

school, 13
set, 11
sister, 9
table, 11
teacher, 15
team, 19
work, 5,
   17, 19

Word Count: 74
Early-Intervention Level: 9

Credits
Mari C. Schuh, editor; Jennifer Schonborn, series designer and illustrator;
Gary Sundermeyer, photographer; Nancy White, photo stylist; Karen Risch, product
planning editor

Pebble Books thanks the Murphy and Polanek families of Chicago, Illinois, for
modeling in this book and Rebecca Glaser of Mankato, Minnesota, for providing
photo shoot locations.

The author dedicates this book to the memory of her grandparents, Willmar and
Janet Schuette.